"Good Morning!" Glory

Rosemary McGraw

A publication of

Eber & Wein Publishing

Pennsylvania

"Good Morning!" Glory

Copyright © 2017 by Rosemary McGraw

Library of Congress
Cataloging in Publication Data

ISBN 978-1-60880-610-2

Proudly manufactured in the United States of America by

Eber & Wein Publishing

Pennsylvania

"Good Morning!" Glory

Adieu

Old Man Winter doffs his
Hat when he meets his lady fair;
Lilacs and white lilies
Adorn her golden hair.

Meeting in a cooling breeze
He feels her warm embrace;
Pausing for a moment
He looks into her face.

One fleeting glance,
One single thought:
"So little time with you,"
Then running with the wind
He bids Miss Spring adieu.

My Babysitter

Who holds me close when Mommy's gone
And tells me Mommy won't be long?   My babysitter.

Who tells me I must learn to say
Please and thank you every day?   My babysitter.

Who cleans the stains from off my dress?
Who tells me she loves me the best
Then softly tucks me in to rest?   My babysitter.

Who tells me I must share my toys?
(but surely not with little boys!)   My babysitter.

Who goes outside with me to play
And wipes the dirt and tears away?   My babysitter.

When I fall down, who comes to see
And sticks Band-Aids all over me?
"Oh, no!" I say, "not there, my knee!"   My babysitter.

Who scolds me when I'm very bad
And talks to me when I am sad?   My babysitter.

Who gives me too much birthday cake
And rocks away my tummy ache?   My babysitter.

So much to do. the hours fly.
"My Mommy's home!" We say goodbye.
What did I hear—was that a sigh?
Of course—   My babysitter.

Blessed Are the Peacemakers

Am I willing to tolerate
Those intolerable?
Am I willing to love
All those unlovable?

When hurts and hasty words
Become part of living,
For each accusation
Can I be forgiving?

If I hear an ugly rumor
Lord, help me put those things behind;
Just keep them to myself
And not invade another's mind.

And if my brother fails,
Lord, help me understand
He doesn't need my good advice,
He needs a helping hand.

Christmas, My Brother and Me

The wind was cold; it stung my ears
and turned my cheeks to red.
A crust of ice covered the ground
beneath my brother's sled.

He pulled the sled beyond the barn
and through the pasture gate.
We left our prints in soft, brown, earth
that gave way to our weight.

We walked trails he walked last
year to look, my brother and me,
the holidays were here and we
needed a Christmas tree.

I wonder why I tagged along,
I guess, so I could be there
to watch the snow fall to the ground
and stick to my brother's hair.

I can't remember wrapping gifts
or putting trim on a tree
but I recall a wooden sled,
Christmas, my brother and me.

Decoration Day

We return to the hills of Appalachia
When the creek below the house is roaring
From spring rains; when moisture hangs heavy
On the trees. Silence is broken by the steady
Beat of dripping, bouncing off the final flight
Of last year's fallen leaves.

Kinfolks come from other states and counties
To reunite the living at the site of loved ones
Laid to rest. Each one carries baskets of food
And fresh cut flowers; some with lilacs and lilies,
Some with roses and gladiolus, some with chicken
And biscuits and strawberry pie.

Because the end of May is Decoration Day.
We return. Everyone. Once a year. Every year.
Like the swallows that return to Capistrano.

The Dance of the Grasshoppers

This is the way it is today
And the way it will always be;
Ants labor and grasshoppers play,
Both want security.

"I have a plan," said the elephant.
"Yes," said the ass, "for the ants.
You can't see grasshoppers," said he,
"They never plan, they dance."

"They too, I'm told, will soon grow old.
Now who do you think will pay
For those who chose
To dance their days away?"

Progress?

Morning sun passed through glass on the door
Fading the carpet I stood on.

Motel litter lay on the terrace floor
Waiting to be walked on.

A sudden thud bounced off the door
Bringing me from places

My thoughts had been before.
To watch a sparrow die in trash
Upon a concrete floor.

He tried to live with man
His grave: a sandwich box
His stone: a cola-can.

El Shaddai

In streams of rippling waters, unhurried, cool and clean;
In forest glades, a resting place, untroubled and serene.

In evenings brilliant colors my gaze is fixed on things above
And across this vast horizon is a reflection of unlimited love.

As rivers rise and winds increase, You offer me security;
When I see nature in Your grip, I see Your all supremacy.

In the faith of a child; in the smile of a friend, in the love between You
    and me;
And the light in the eyes of a dear old saint—I see Your divinity.

You are everywhere, in everything, in all things good and kind;
My omnipotent, omniscient, omnipresent God—

You have captured my heart and my mind.

Emerald Isle

When will the leaves return again
to dance upon my tree;
Like fairies on an emerald isle
They swayed so gracefully.

I watched them twirl and pirouette,
Much like a French ballet;
They entertained me many hours
Throughout the summers day.

One day their costumes changed
From green to red and gold;
This was their grand finale
And soon the air turned cold.

They dances until they danced no more;
They twirled and twirled around
And one by one my fairy leaves
Fell softly to the ground.

They rest beneath the snow,
I cannot count their number;
The tree and I are standing by
Throughout their night of slumber.

To wait until they dance again
And wave to me and smile,
Twirl and dip and pirouette
Like fairies on an emerald isle.

Evidence Seen

You love me not because
You are expected to
But because you just want to.

You never expect more from me
Than you are willing to give.

You let me follow with dignity
Until I can lead with humility.

You have an inner strength, a sense of peace
That exudes a calming influence
On all those around you.

You are always in tune with needs
Of others, seeing things buried
Beneath the surface—

You hear the roar of words unspoken,
Of feelings wrapped in silence---yet
You always understand.

You are the top of the mountain
And the reason I climb.

Forever the Same

Between creator and creation
A gulf too wide, too great, to span
Until through one called Jesus
The great I AM became a man.

His words, the very thoughts of God,
Suddenly human—near at hand
To speak as simply as we speak
Words you and I can understand.

Should all the stars evaporate
And rivers cease to flow,
Should mountains fall into the sea
He will remain the same—you know.

Infallible, unchangeable,
Always ever available,
When we see faith and values flee
That's when He says, "Just trust in me."

February 5, 2010

Forgive

Lord, help me to forgive,
Set my spirit free;
Loose the bonds that separate
A loving God from me.

Oh, God of mercy, lift my guilt
From all hostility;
Root out all resentment,
Anger and anxiety.

It isn't easy to forget
But can I not forgive?
Instead, I dredge up hurts
To relive and relive.

I keep them all inside,
No peace to ever know,
Bitterness creeps in because
I cannot let them go.

Will vengeance heal my heart
Or give me peace of mind?
Will it mend a world torn apart
Or give to me a will to find

A way to break the barriers
Between You, Lord, and me;
Remind me, please, the many times
You have forgiven me.

Four and No More

In a cottage built for four,
room enough for four and no more.
Behind a fence with an iron gate,
lived Meg, her parents and sister, Kate.

Neighbors who came were asked to wait
on the other side of the iron gate.
"We care for our own," Pop said to Kate,
"no time for those beyond the gate."

The fragrant smell of the piney wood
gave him a life he thought was good,
then sparks set fire to the cottage floor
and no one came from the house next door.

They saw the smoke in the piney wood
and the slab of stone where the cottage stood.
They tried to help but had to wait
on the other side of the iron gate.

A Hush

Hangs over the darkness
As I lie beneath the moon;
Drifting waters whisper
In my sleepy lagoon.

Warm, summer air
Is blessed by a tune
When night creatures
Begin to croon.

The cares of the day,
Removed from sight,
By lullabies
That sing in the night.

Like a baby, He holds
Me close to His breast;
Curtains are drawn,
I am tucked in to rest.

My mind is at rest,
My heart is in tune
And I am at peace
In my sleepy lagoon.

Lord, Will You Walk with Me?

When I weary from this journey,
Lord, will you walk with me?
When the burdens grow heavy,
Will You carry them for me?

When I give up and stop praying
For answers I can't wait to see;
When I replace my faith and trust
With insecurity;

When I forget Your ways
Have always been the best for me;
Let me sense Your presence
And feel Your hand on me.

Forgive me, Lord, my faith is weak,
I know I don't deserve to be
The object of so great a love
That only You can offer me.

Love Me the Way I Am

Whether you see me as
sinner or saint,
Love me the way I am
and not the way I ain't.

Sometimes I am thoughtless,
before I look I leap.
Seeds I sow I shouldn't
sow I, also, have to reap.

I need to learn to listen
but before too long
My feet are in my mouth,
not where my feet belong.

I hurt when I am hurt,
the same as any one of you.
I make mistakes doing
things I should never do.

Until I have grown
into what I should be,
I really don't know how
to be anyone but me.

An Interlude

Barefoot in weeds still wet with dew
In early mornings breeze;
Pelicans stand on oyster beds
Beneath the mangrove trees.

They fish awhile and feed awhile
And watch the sun of morning rise;
I watch the ever moving tide
And track the path the osprey flies.

Sweeping low across the harbor
Is independence on display,
The pride of every patriot
Waits on the seawall in the bay.

Soon the flutter of his wings
Takes him high above the swaying frond
To soar through shades of orange
And blue into the vast beyond.

Oh—that I could put on hold
The ticking away of my days;
No people to meet, no schedules to keep,
Content to be a pawn of praise.

Ladora Belle

A name that rings with laughter,
makes the heart a little lighter, but
what should have been was not.
Trapped by tradition
and the culture of her time
in a union not of her making.
Was it her acceptance
hiding in a long print dress?
What was torn beneath her apron?

Did this quiet resignation
cause the sadness in her eyes
most would never see beneath a bonnet?
Did grandpa's death
increase the load she carried?
or was her compensation
independence?
Slow to speak and slow to anger
the only grandma I remember
went away when I was just a girl.

Mother

The sun is warm
a beam of light
sends rays across the room;
I lift my head
from where I sit
I see the roses bloom.

A splash of red
upon each breast
their fragrance fills the room;
inside my book
a rose pressed tight
has lost its sweet perfume.

An empty pew,
a hymnal worn,
the organ pumps a tune;
among the reds
my rose is white
so much is gone so soon.

Through change,
through loss, I feel
such comfort in this room
because I know
my faded rose,
somewhere, is still in bloom.

A Moment of Peace

Did His hand brush my cheek,
a touch and then no more,
or was it just a breeze? Where were
the thoughts I had before?

A touch, a sigh, my troubled
mind found a sweet release;
like soothing balm the gentle
breeze softly whispered peace.

From puffs to gales the breeze
and I are moved by too much force.
Is this when we lose our way
and veer, too far, off course?

I wish I knew but when it comes
that wind, in time, will cease
and once again the gentle breeze
will softly whisper peace.

October Story

What can compare to October
When leaves turn red and gold?
The Master scatters the paint
And we watch the beauty unfold.

After the chill and killing frost,
They fall, one by one, to the earth.
Their reason for being is incomplete,
They wait for the day of rebirth.

Dying makes way for the living,
Sustaining them all winter through.
New life comes forth in spring
And the cycle begins anew.

Will I be a source of strength
For those that follow me
Or will you have to push your way
Through all of my debris?

Will my living be a blessing,
A pleasing memory;
My dying an inspiration
and peace my legacy?

Has my life served a purpose,
Will I give God the glory?
His handiwork is told
In October's story.

Old Glory

Tears in my eyes and a lump in my throat
As I watch the raising of the flag. I see the stars
And stripes draped over caskets of those who gave
Their life so I can live free. I see her in the house
Of God, in the halls of congress, on hats, on
Homes, in automobiles and in most
Public schools.

Stained at Bunker Hill, shot through
At Gettysburg and hung in shreds on Iwo
Jima. Faded and frayed, she went with the brave
From there to Pork Chop Hill. Unfolding her colors
She marched through the jungles of Nam, through
The old and smut of Kuwait to be tossed in
Closets and chest of drawers to wait
For a day like today.

Towers tumbled. The world watched
As the strong and silent rose from the dust
And rubble to lift her as high as she had
Been lifted before. Old Glory was needed
Once more.

Oops!

To be the main attraction was
not my plan for the day;
I didn't know I had to face
a briefcase in the way.

The floor came up to meet
me, looking up from where I lay,
I thought, Oh Lord!
this, too will pass away.

I heard them snicker as
they dropped their head.
I felt my burning cheeks
and knew my face was red.

One moment in memory
Time will never erase;
A loud hurrah and then they said,
"We like your style and grace."

Procrastination

Have I settled into
A place of my own choosing?
No adventure—no surprises—
I wonder what I'm losing?

Thinking makes me weary,
My mind has gone to sleep;
I neither plant nor do I water
Nor have I helped to feed the sheep.

Contented with "what is"
Has been easy for me;
To set aside—or just ignore
The call of what "might be."

Psalms 84

"My soul is longing for the courts."
His flesh cried out for God
To meet for adoration
Where blessed ones had trod.

David's sickness was upon him,
It was God that he yearned for;
Weeping, pleading for the privilege
To find a little more.

Embraced by His presence
When saints were gathered round;
Like a magnet he was drawn
To walk on hallowed ground.

Beneath the temple eaves
The swallows built their nest;
Even they were envied
For their chosen place of rest.

I understand the hunger
The psalmist had to bear
For no one loves the house of God
Like the one who can't be there.

Solitude

Beneath a canopy of green
my life begins anew
where yesterday is washed away
with early morning dew.

In stillness there is pleasure,
for me, beyond compare.
Fragrance from the pine seems
to permeate the air.

Logs were meant for sitting;
no greater comfort can be found
than to rest my feet in carpet
formed by moss upon the ground.

Violets blooming by the brook
are there to pick if I want to;
instead, they stretch their heads
to light that filters through.

Above a flowing stream
with nothing else to do,
dragonflies catch sunlight
through wings of green and blue.

In the thicket I can hear
the rustling of the leaves
and around the honeysuckle
the buzzing of the bees.

Bushy tails and cotton
tails stop to say hello.
Above me in the trees,
slowly, floating on the breeze,
the sweet, sweet, song of the sparrow.

Reveille

The house of God lies sleeping
Upon a barren shore;
Are we apathetic
Because we watch no more?

Has His word been so twisted
We are filled with doubt?
Did complacency set in because
We threw His Bible out?

Has life of too much plenty
Increased our years of slumber?
Can we see the blind ones
Growing greater in number?

How long are we going to sleep?
How long until we count the cost?
How many of our loved ones
Are still among the lost?

How long until we pray
For revival from within?
How long until the light
Of glory shines for us again?

A River, Great

A river as great as boulders are old
Created a little stream
To tumble down the mountain
And rest where shepherds dream.

Bouncing bubbles whispered
In the early morning steam
And diamonds danced in sunlight
On the surface of the stream.

Angry wind—piercing rain—
Destruction so extreme,
The debris upon the water
Denied access to the stream.

The river, great, broke through
The damn with power to redeem;
Restoration! Liberation!
From the source to the stream.

Something had been added
That made the rippling waters teem;
The sound of peace unending
Flowing in the little stream.

Service?

Am I ready, Lord, to serve You?
Have I been purified?
Am I, now, a vessel empty
With room for You inside?

Do I love as You have loved me,
Reaching those unjustified?
But can my faith sustain the wait
As saints of old have testified?

Can I let go of me and say:
"Dear Lord, I'll step aside?"
Will I follow as You lead,
Will I accept You as my guide?

If this is more than sweet communion
And with You I'm crucified
Will I, then, speak with assurance:
"Let my Lord be magnified?"

Scaredy Cat

There was no sleep for me, what I needed was some air;
Near the window I could hear the rhythmic rocking of my chair.

The ticking of the clock said, "Look, it's half-past one,"
Another day was over, a new day had begun.

The wind was shuffling leaves and thunder—off, somewhere;
The darkness seemed to magnify my creaking rocking chair.

Stillness closed around me, my skin—as damp as the air—
Did I hear something or someone creeping up the outside stair?

Afraid to move—a boom! A crack! A flash of light!
Uncovered my intruder tip-toeing in the night.

Upon my feet, I crossed the room to let the stranger in;
Around, around, my feet he twirled, I felt so foolish when

I saw he was a dear old friend. He jumped on the bed in a leap;
Soon he and I were fast asleep. The end.

Talk to Me!

How do I cross a deep so vast
It keeps outsiders out?
Across oceans of indifference
To build trust where there is doubt?

Across the seas of ignorance
To learn the reasons why
A lack of understanding
Exists for you and I.

Across narrow-minded mountains
Where almost any man can find
Seeds of bigotry to sow
In the hearts of all mankind.

Across this barren wilderness
Let there be communication;
Then lessons learned from living past
Could bless a future generation.

So much beauty, truth and wisdom
We could be sharing with each other
If we understood the benefits
Of loving one another.

Tattered Sweater

I didn't like the way he dressed,
I knew he knew better;
What would people think
Of his old tattered sweater.

I didn't like the places
That he chose to go,
I didn't like the people
That he chose to know,

I could make him over
Into someone better
But first I would replace
His old tattered sweater.

I took him from the places
That he chose to go
And far from every friend
That he chose to know.

His life was empty then,
His friends were those I chose;
They didn't know the man
Beneath those polished clothes.

I looked through tears and saw
Anew this one dear to me;
How could I have been so blind
To not see what I see.

Who was I to try to fit
This man into my mold;
Who was I to make over
One God made into Gold.

I wiped away my tears
And returned his sweater,
He smiled and walked away
Knowing he had made me better.

Time to Wait

Teach me to wait, Lord, slow me down.
Remind me I am made of clay,
When I worry too much tell me
If nothing gets done—it's okay.

As I leave my room this morning
Grant me the grace to wait,
Still a too busy mind
And slow a hurried gait.

With all eternity in mind,
There is time to chat with a friend;
To find peace in falling snowflakes
And solitude in each days end.

Time to think on heaven's glories,
"Amazing Grace" will lift me up;
Alone—shut in—I wait
For You to fill an empty cup.

Trusting the Lord

When the clouds part
and the sun peeks through,
when light is the brightest,
and anxieties few,

when faith has tomorrow
clearly in view,
I trust Him for me,
and I trust Him for you.

When the sun slips away
with the waning light,
I trust Him to lead me
all through the night.

When trouble torments me,
and my portion is pain,
I trust Him again
and again and again.

As my days and my weeks
add up to a year,
I have learned it is better
to trust than to fear.

For no life is sweeter
than to claim the reward,
of living a life, just
trusting the Lord.

This Morning Was Mine

The wind blew all day and night, sweeping
The valley clean. Large balls of dry tumbleweed
Bounced across the terrain. Trash cans rolled
Down the hill, their lids spinning in air, as
Helpless as a leaf in a rushing stream.

By dawn a brown landscape was white.
Nothing moved. Not even a jackrabbit.
The cold air of morning met me in the stillness.
It seemed I could hear the beating of my heart.
A mirage of opaque colors danced on the surface
Until they were captured by a cloud. Naked
Limbs that groaned all night were covered
With a blanket as soft as my cotton gown.

Steam from the valley circled the mountain
As huge chunks of snow fell onto boulders
Of red granite; a refuge as old as earth itself.
Cooling, melting, snow seeped through trees
Unable to grow gave drink to a sun-baked land.

A Trucker's Lament

Four wheelers to the left of him, one glued to the right headlight;
Another crossed in front of him from the far left to the right.
He slammed the brakes, the big rig shook, throwing log sheets in the air;
The trucker trembled—he knew—he held it with a prayer.
With pedal to the metal the big rig left them there.
And the compact kamikaze was heard to yell, "Unfair!"
Cold coffee leaped from mugs staining carpet on the floor;
His eyes aflame like two hot coals, the trucker screamed: "No More!"
Down the Wasatch Mountains he dodged the gators snare;
Like flies around a chip, those little cars were everywhere!
"I will get you," yelled the trucker, "if it takes until I die,
All you can do is aggravate the big rigs you pass by."
His features were distorted in a demonic way;
Maybe—he thought—today will be the day.

Until Spring Comes Again

Morning breezes woke me as curtains brushed my face;
The sweet smell of lilacs made this a moment to embrace.
Bright rays of light streaming from the risen sun
Fell across my pillow before my day had, yet, begun.
In awe, I stood... not sure how long...

To watch the mallards on the wing;
And hear the chirrup song the little blue birds sing
An over abundance of afternoon showers
Cooled the earth with His touch to dress up the flowers.
He changed the leaves from green to red to gold to brown;
Soon, wood smoke and fire spread laughter all over town.

The brisk biting days of Autumn tend to quicken my pace;
I paused to look at the blush He painted on your face.
Sleet peppered my windows, my walls kept the wind at bay;
Frigid, bone-chilling cold turned bright blue skies to gray.
So happy to have no place to go when the wind chill is ten below;
Nothing much to do but wait and watch the falling snow.

Until Spring comes again...

Walking Backwards

Walking backwards is unnatural
Because everyone knows
You cannot keep your balance with
Your heels before your toes.

Looking backwards is unnatural,
Why—if your head is turned that way
You will bump into tomorrow
And never see today.

You need to see what is because
What was is now has been;
Just put your heels behind your toes
And go forward again.

Set your sites toward the future,
That is the natural way;
You will always have tomorrow
To think of yesterday.

We Need Each Other

At half-past three school was out, Johnnie hurried down
To the pet shop on the corner near the edge of town.

As faithful as the clock that hung upon the wall
He worked to feed the pets without reward at all.

Mr. Miller said to Johnnie, "You don't need to be alone.
It seems to me you'd want to have a puppy of your own."

"Oh, I would," he replied, "I'd like that very much
But I have no money—your puppies cost too much.

"Nonsense boy!" he answered, "odd jobs can be found,
You can earn the money if you go ask around."

Johnnie missed his little friends, now he spent his time
Cutting grass, raking leaves and saving every dime.

At last, he had enough. He ran to the edge of town
To the pet shop on the corner and laid his money down.

"Excuse me, Mr. Miller, I want a puppy of my own.
You know the one I mean, he spends his time alone."

"Oh no!" said Mr. Miller, "he was crippled in a fall.
He cannot fetch a stick or run with you to chase a ball."

But Johnnie reached inside the cage, "I will not take another,
Look!" said he, "I have a brace on this leg and the other;
I am crippled, too. You see, we need each other."

When Winter's Gone

Youth now spent, I recall
The wintry winds and blowing snow.
Much older now, I am surprised
To find I miss it so.

I look up as if to see
the leaves just hanging on;
And watch the tree set them free
To soar to parts unknown.

Listening to their rustle
As they race across the lawn;
Too soon the wind will pick them up
And then the leaves are gone.

When winter winds blow through
The trees, it is a wailing cry;
In hearing, I can feel the pain
Of cold bare limbs against the sky.

Trees that had given shade
Could shelter no one, now.
They looked like bones of dead
Men, yet, they lived...somehow.

I saw myriads of colors dancing
As sunlight hit the fallen snow
Like a hundred children prancing
Until the wind began to blow.

So, send your thoughts to rest in me,
Each one I will borrow;
Though, I am here and you are there
Each one I will follow.

Then I, here in my sunny place
Will remember long ago;
The wood fires warm embrace
When winter winds began to blow.

Publishing Credits

The National Library of Poetry—Owings Mills, MD
The Write Technique—New York, NY
The Sparrowgrass Poetry—Sistersville, WV
Southern Poetry Association—Pass Christian, MS
National Arts Society—Pass Christian, MS
The Iliad Press—Troy, MI
The Nuthouse Magazine—Ellenton, FL
Feather Books—Shropshire, UK
The Tale Spinners—Alberta, CANADA
Pickle Gas Press (The Aardvark Adventurer)—Penfield, NY
Country Folk Magazine—Pittsburgh, PA
Time for Rhyme—Battleford, SK Canada
The inkwell—Katy, TX
Hodge Podge—Springfield, MO
The Plowman Ministries—Ontario, Canada
The Society of American Poets (The Poet's Pen)—Macon, GA
The Storyteller—Maynard, OR
Horse Latitude Press—Rhododendron, OR
Poetic License (Mikashef Enterprises)—Yucca Valley, CA
Creativity Unlimited—Rancho Palos Verdes, CA
RBS Poets View Point, Eunice, NM
The Shepherd—Rock Island, IL
Eber & Wein Publishing—New Freedom, PA

9 781608 806102